As If Through a Window

Mia Burrus

Welcome...

Is this a memoir? Perhaps not. Like all writing, it is a voyage of discovery, an investigation of things at once universal and particular to my time, place, body, mind, family, fortunes, ideas, thoughts, images, and memories. The memories are mine, but the text is only incidentally about me.

These intertwined narratives, in a mix of genres and media, are about my father, Étienne Burrus, and the cattle ranch that occupied him for half his life.

As If Through a Window

My mother, a Montrealer, never liked Calgary, though she could have been unhappy anywhere as it turned out. When she left my father, she took us girls back east in 1964 and we were left looking at our bits of life in Alberta as if through a window.

I don't know who took this photograph of my father in 1975; it's not mine. I know I kept it because of the small story—comment even—that accompanied it and made it memorable. Its import was affirmed thirty years later when my father's obituary was accompanied by another photo of him wearing a cowboy hat.

This lovely image, so the story goes, shows him smiling, slightly tipsy, relieved that the June branding weekend at the ranch, which started uncertainly, had turned out right. Much like the dream he brought from France—the iconic image of the west, the wide prairie, freedom, tethered horses, city friends, placid cattle, challenge, big sky filled with fair-weather clouds—had turned out right.

Unseen is the dirty, smoky, smelly work of branding the bawling calves. Unseen is my own absence. My sister and I were not invited to come from Toronto, where we lived with our mother, for branding weekend, much as we craved that promise of excitement. Our window on ranch life, on this constant in our experience of our father's life, was the relative peace of summer vacation, when the soundscape of the prairie was buzzing flies and wind-sighing grass. We were tourists in our father's life.

Five Cents

I've collected many stories from many people —about my father, about the ranch—and am puzzled about how to get at the truth when it's different for everyone. It's like having a pocket full of nickels. You put your hand in, and they all feel the same, but when you pull them out and examine them, you see slight differences in age, lustre, abrasion, sometimes country of origin. The oldest of them have twelve edges, twelve angles! But you have asked for their stories, and they've been proffered with the expectation that you will take them at face value. Getting below the surface is a challenge; I settle for shiny adjectives. I am more accustomed to writing poetry, to the "Ars Poetica", as described by Archibald MacLeish in his poem of the same name, to writing that is "Dumb/As old medallions to the thumb."

When we were children, we would often amuse ourselves at the ranch with an antique slot machine. You would feed the thing a nickel and pull the arm, hoping for pay-dirt, but having to settle for fruit salad. When we ran out of nickels we opened a door at the back, scooped out the nickels, and played again, hoping for life as a bowl of cherries, even as life served up lemons. As with all gamblers, we wanted our paltry investment to return an oracular, splendid truth.

Tell me, o one-armed bandit, what is the meaning of all these five-cent facts?

We come by way of yesterday

on the lookout for tomorrow,

ill-attending the heartbeat at hand,

the technicolour present, the sounds

that don't stay, the breeze

on your face that sets you

in space, and then, oh, that scent—

point-blank to your memory bank,

sending you with your heavy

pack to collect

that crusted coin

that still shines for you.

Mr. B.

I first knew my grandparents' house in Ste. Croix, a small village in Alsace, as a small child, which means I only knew aspects of it, corners of it, knew it less as infrastructure than as bits of theatre sets for small dramas. Memories of the sharp crunching gravel walks and drives that tore my knee open when I fell off a bike at speed vie with the small, lovely breakfast room where my sisters and I were served Crêpes Suzette despite our childish inelegance. I returned, middle-aged, old enough to be not only appreciative but impressed, to tour the empty house as part of a family reunion.

The kitchen was large and spare, almost institutional, little changed from when it was designed to serve a grand house built in the 1930s. High on the wall in the kitchen were labeled lights that would alert the domestic staff that one of the family had rung. Monsieur, Madame, Anne-Marie, Françoise, Martin, Bernard, René, Mr. B., Agnès. Mr. B.? That was the youngest boy, my father, Étienne. How he came to be called Mr. B. is lost to time, but it became a convenient handle when he moved to Alberta, where the French language was considered, at best, unnecessary, and a name like Étienne Burrus could create awkward moments, aahs and ehs, invented pronunciations and mis-stressed syllables chewed and spat out.

(His middle name was beyond consideration. Hubert: in French it rhymes with Pooh Bear, in English it conjures a large wind instrument glimpsed at the back of an orchestra.)

Once while visiting a fishing camp on New Brunswick's Miramichi and being introduced to the proprietor, someone he'd never meet again, he offered his hand and interjected "Ed". Ed? Did he forget he was in a bilingual province, or now being older and hard of hearing, just take the path of least resistance? Why not "Stephen", his name in English? This had never been an option.

Étienne was Mr. B. on the ranch, Mr. B. to the grown children of his wife Kay, to those with whom he was fondly familiar. Mr. B. was well-known to others, but a mystery to me.

An Absence

D ivorces were less common when I was a child, due in part to the difficulty of obtaining one. Society created, even legislated, great pressure on the marital home. Some became pressure cookers.

I did not know how to answer friends' questions about why my parents got divorced. It was certainly my mother's initiative. Once, I scratched with a stone the word 'coward' on the bricks of a neighbour's garage. My mother had thus labelled my father once—but what did it mean? I would guess now that it was my father's propensity to walk away from a fight. A fight with my mother or a fight on her behalf? I don't know why this was the only answer I had at the time.

I had to ask my mother what Dad did for a living. "Say he's a businessman," she said. Another meaningless term. This time it was my elementary school teacher who had asked. Each of us in class were called up to the teacher's desk to answer a few questions, one of which was father's occupation. I don't know why these questions were asked and the answers recorded, how they were useful to the administration of our education, unless it was some kind of stealthy social work. The assumption, of course, was that the father was part of the home and that what he did all day was common knowledge.

A businessman conducted business. Circular and self-referential. This pat answer was a purposeful or apathetic means of not knowing our father. And so, what did it mean to be told "you're just like your father!"

What did I learn from the father who didn't teach me? His lessons might not have been overt, but they infiltrated my DNA, like a virus.

I learned how to make a classic salad dressing, to sing classic campfire songs, how to at least read French from his childhood picture books, how to ski at least down the baby hill, how to install electrical fixtures, how to check a house's foundation using a marble, and that you don't want to live a literal stone's throw from a school. He told us that it's impolite to talk about money, politics or religion, though such brush-offs could also have been a means of not knowing our father, or that he stood for nothing.

When my parents separated, still in Calgary, I was too young to understand. Like most children of divorced parents, my father became the 'amusement dad'. He took us skiing, to the Ice Capades and the circus. I remember watching the clock in the kitchen, waiting for him for what seemed to be a painfully long time, until being redirected to watch the minute hand instead of the hour hand!

I associate the separation and the temporary move to a drab apartment with cold war anxiety. Jets flew overhead, breaking the sound barrier, silent but for the sonic boom. The civil defense warnings that were broadcast on the TV—

"this is a test; it is only a test"— even the TV's pre-broadcast test pattern had a rigid and ominous look. I remember, too, my mother's panic at seeing some child's mangled bike being put into the trunk of a police car —was it mine? This was the general feeling of insecurity that seeped in after my mother's daring break with tradition.

And when we were to leave Calgary, the prairies, and Dad and move to Toronto, I hid behind the living room drapes, clutching his photo and crying at the baseless thought of never seeing him again. My mother found me and cried, too, unable to comfort me.

Making a Killing

"I hear the buffalo hoofs pounding in their stomachs."

Louise Halfe Sky-Dancer,

To say that tens of millions of buffalo *(Bison bison)* vanished from the prairies in the late eighteen-hundreds is to whitewash a slaughter of historical proportions. American hunters sparked a demand for bison hides for use as machine belts, which Canadian hunters filled in their turn. The bison carcasses were left to rot; their skeletons littered the plains.

When the Canadian Pacific Railroad (CPR) was completed in the late eighteen-hundreds, its first eastbound cargo was those bison bones. They were collected by settlers, who needed to clear them off their new homesteads, and by anyone else, young or old, who wanted to make a bit of cash. They were carted to the rail line and piled as much as fifteen feet high, stretching along the track for up to a mile. Pile of Bones, a canvas town that sprang up where the railroad crossed Wascana Creek in the North-West Territory, was eventually given the more dignified name of Regina, Saskatchewan.

Those bones, rendered, burnt, or powdered were traded to

make bone china. Sugar refiners and wineries found bison bone ash polished sugar and clarified wine better than did wood ash. But most of the bones were ground into bonemeal fertilizer and put back onto the denuded land. The supply of bones diminished, and within twenty years was depleted; the prairie fell silent; no thunder but from summer storms.

Siksika, Piikani, Tsuut'ina, Stoney-Nakoda, Kainai nations— they had followed the bison herds, from which they made their living, later making use of weapons and horses traded from European adventurers. By 1879, adventurers from the new nations of Canada and the United States had nearly exterminated the bison and by doing so deliberately collapsed the First Nations' ancient economy. Famine forced thousands onto the new reserves. Then their hunting grounds were bisected by the railroad. In anticipation of these 'economic' changes on the one hand, and the need for land for the railroad on the other, and the ensuing struggles over both, Treaty 7 was signed with the Crown in 1877 to bring peace to the prairie. The treaty guaranteed that the nations' traditional, free life would continue, and the rest of their ancestral lands were surrendered to the Crown. It then transferred jurisdiction to the government of Canada, with the understanding that Canada would meet the Crown's treaty obligations to the nations—promises hollowed out over time, promises that 'vanished' like the bison.

Buffalo Alberta

The wind and the railroad
pinned you to a point on a line
on a plane. On a plain
where space stretched out time
there was no hurry.

B uffalo Alberta had a population of three in 1991: the
teacher, the postmistress, and her husband. There was
a school, a grain elevator, a tiny church, a post office;

everything else was boarded up or torn down. Soon enough these buildings would be gone, even the prairie sentinel—the grain elevator.

The average population density of the area is now one person for every five square miles. Five square miles of Manhattan averages 364,000 inhabitants.

How can I convey on such a small page the sweep of a place that yet supports so few? The ranch my father established in 1969, Majestic Ranches Ltd., covered 26,000 acres, anchored at one corner by Buffalo, Alberta. Back then, there was a farmstead in the western part of the ranch known as the upper buildings, and a miscellany of structures called the lower buildings, scattered on the bottom lands of the Red Deer River, liquid gold that flowed along the ranch's eastern boundary. It was a twenty-minute drive from upper to lower, long-distance to talk on the telephone between the two, sixteen miles to spend an evening with the nearest neighbour.

As I write, I am travelling by train through northern Ontario, where the human population may be as sparse as the ranch, yet the trackless tangle of trees and lakes do not suggest the emptiness of the semi-desert. I imagine hidden eyes watching the train slide by.

At the ranch, electric poles or even a rancher standing in a field can dominate the landscape, like sentinels. But the land is not as flat as imagined. Once the ocean bottom, it undulates like the sea, rolls gently enough that you can walk over a seemingly insubstantial hummock and lose sight of the few landmarks you have been noting from the corner of your eye. Then where are you?

The dun-coloured deer blend with the dun-coloured grass, only visible once they dart away, impelled in one direction or another by a whiff on the breeze. Crowning it all, the big sky; the summertime sky brilliantly blue and sprouting fair weather clouds as the day warms—the winter sky a grey blanket. If you are up before dawn and step outside, the great dome is a map of bright stars, which, over the sea of grass, says "you are here"; does not say "this is the way to go." The six dim stars you might see in Manhattan would have nothing to say to you if you took note of them at all above the noise of city lights.

In summer, the aurora borealis might reach down into the southern Alberta night as sheer white curtains wafting spectrally in an unfelt electromagnetic breeze. But in winter, the bitter nights might blaze with the crackling full colour play of northern lights, a celestial gift for the hardy and persistent who might be out for a silent night walk.

Silence. How many settlers in the early nineteen-hundreds disappeared into the prairie on offer, only later to disappear into the prairie unknown, defeated by the earth and its invisible curtain of woe, the clouds that will not deliver rain?

The Palliser Triangle

In 2005, following the worst drought on record, twenty inches of rain fell on the ranch. Ranchers and cows alike thought they'd died and gone to heaven.

By the time the CPR was completed in 1885, only twenty-three homesteads had been claimed along the four hundred miles from Moose Jaw, Saskatchewan to Calgary, Alberta. Captain John Palliser, a British government surveyor, had surveyed the area in 1859 and deemed much of the area a semi-desert unfit for agriculture. But at the turn of the century, it flashed its green riches for a few wet years, blinding all who saw it to its true nature, and the prairie filled with new immigrants. Then it dwindled back to its usual dry dullness. By the nineteen-thirties many homesteaders had walked away from their farms.

This is not a land of averages. Human ingenuity attempts to smooth the extremes. Sowing and irrigating silage crops extend the grazing season without stressing the native grasses.

Still, rain years are a cowboy's heaven where lush grasses and quiet cattle stretch to where the blue sky meets the horizon. Prickly-pear cactus and wild roses flower. But when it is dry, even a rabbit hopping over a hill would raise puffs of dust. Many who settled and then left this land, watched the sky darken to slate, and the rain hang like a soft grey veil never reaching the ground.

Driving the prairie's two-lane roads, the abundant wildlife—the partridges, long-billed curlew, pheasant, grouse, red fox, antelope, deer, elk, bald eagles, wild turkey, prairie rattlesnakes, coyotes—were not as apparent as the rancher's struggle—the work, worry, thirsty crops, grasses withering, cattle prices plunging, grasshoppers, drought followed by a hard winter. The uninitiated saw sky, sagebrush, gophers, dust. Those who lived there knew there was an under-the-radar profusion of life, grounded as the deep-rooted grasses, subtle as the wind gently lifting the golden stems.

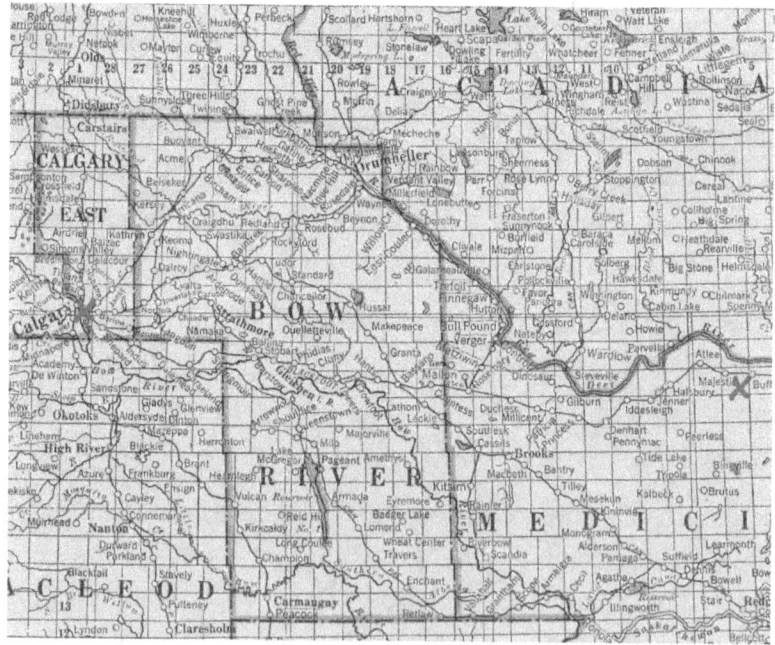

Southern Alberta 1942

Leaving Alsace

O n the other side of the world, the myth of the west still sparked dreams of adventure and fortune.

Étienne was born in 1927 in Ste. Croix-aux-Mines, a village of two thousand souls, one of the many silver mining and textile towns in the Vosges Mountains of Alsace, France. He grew up in a house now known as Villa Burrus (though it's no longer in the family) on a road called Rue Maurice Burrus.

He was the sixth of seven children and the youngest of four boys. The oldest son's path was determined at birth; he would be one of a quadrumvirate of cousins who ran the family firm, F.J. Burrus & Cie, SA., whose early origins in tobacco have since diversified into consumer goods. As the youngest, Étienne was not thus constrained but still felt himself restricted by class—not oppressed in the way the serving and labouring classes were, they who sought freedom in the new world—but imprisoned by strictures of status and appearance. The North American west had inspired dreams of freedom among European society and its hide-bound social hierarchies. Étienne imagined a life in its wide-open spaces, stripped of history, far from family.

He started out in Nancy, France, studying medicine, but was susceptible to pneumonia and advised not to pursue the profession. He then went further afield to Britain to learn English. He eventually acquiesced to his father's advice that he become a banker, and in 1951 travelled further still, to McGill University in Montreal to study Economics. If he had compromised by choosing a place, however far away, that was at least francophone, he was not prepared for the discovery that the Québécois spoke a French that he could barely comprehend. Once settled at McGill, he soon decided that Economics had nothing to teach him and he switched to Geophysics, having determined that oil was not only the business of the future, but a path to the west.

Étienne's childhood ended with the Second World War. Alsace had been disputed territory in many wars, yanked back and forth between Germany and France. The Germans annexed Alsace in 1940, forbade the French language, took over management of the family's tobacco factory in Ste. Croix, and billeted the German company director in the family home. The new director, wondering how to design a new cigarette package, asked Étienne's father, André, who maliciously suggested the Croix de Lorraine, symbol of French and especially Alsatian resistance. Needless to say, the cigarettes bearing the *emblème gaulliste* were a big success with the Alsatians. Not long after, André found it prudent to take advantage of his Swiss citizenship to leave with the family for Lausanne, Switzerland for the duration of the war.

Sharp wits, and their gleeful deployment, ran in the family. Don't get mad, get even, then leave, wait, return with your laurel leaves in your back pocket.

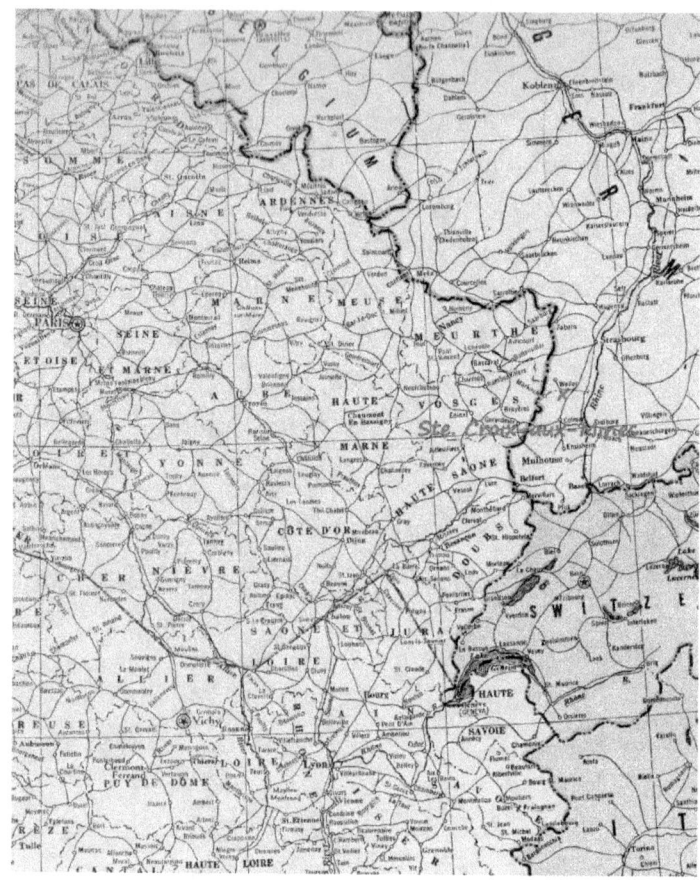

Occupied France 1942

Oise & Mimi: A Fiction

I can tell you that the post card, addressed to *Ma Chère Oise*, and signed with kisses by Mimi, was written in spring 1930 when Oise (Françoise) was fifteen and her sister Mimi (Anne-Marie) was sixteen and Étienne was not quite three.

The ink, still sharply blue eighty years on, the fine hand, and perfect spelling evoke a well-appointed room, spring-scented, away from the nursery noise and clutch of younger brothers.

Oise and Mimi—a fictional interlude

Mimi:

It's lonely with Françoise away. I occupy my time with Étienne, my little doll. He is such a lively and clever one, incapable of telling a fib! He posed so nicely while his picture was taken...I had trimmed his unruly curls...and if the print turns out well, I will send it to ma *chère* Oise, *ma petite oiseau*, with the latest news.

I love my brothers, most of the time...I have so many of them after all...but miss my sister the most. We are only one year apart, like twins really, and like twins we know each other inside out; we need each other's opinions, points of view, and advice. We laugh together in our rooms...when we tire of being dutiful daughters, sometimes we're fit to burst!

Oh, what a life...what will it bring? I have only to look at Mama, of course. She is a saint; I'll never be as pious. I pray my meagre faith can sustain me, or that I'll be blessed with a husband more like *Oncle Pierre*, one who understands the value of a ready smile. Oise and I imagine perfect *beaux*, a double wedding, happy homes in towns not far apart. Her husband will be her opposite in looks, fair and blue-eyed. Mine will likewise have dark hair and eyes in contrast to mine. Our children will be a perfect *mélange* of fair and dark, and when we all come to visit in the summer, Mama will laugh trying to tell the one's children from the other's, and we will laugh to see Papa sternly shepherd them all to keep to the paths of his treasured gardens.

Now look, *Oiseau*, where my thoughts have gone with you not here to keep the sparkle in my eyes. I need your sharp sight and sharper wit to keep me from contemplation of what might be. Our world is small, Strasbourg far away, Paris farther still. The future...once I didn't give it a thought...today was all that mattered...but now that we are out of the nursery, we are adrift, all our choices now made and approved with an eye to the future. Tennis is to be perfected, not enjoyed, the flowers from the garden prized over those of the meadow, the piano played with a smile more serene than silly. We drift from one pastime to the other while our bicycles dim under the attic's dust.

Come home soon, Françoise! (I know, of course, you do.) I can't bear my own and only company for long!

Oise:

My youngest brother, Étienne, has returned; that is, he was here for a few days, and now has gone off to the coast to visit Bernard, leaving his young family behind to partake of our summer ritual—visiting the grandparents, *Bonmama* and *Bonpapa*.

Étienne was only nine when Mimi died, and she was a little mama to him, but did he have to name his daughter Anne-Marie? It's been almost thirty years that she's been dead, and now Papa looks at this little Anne-Marie, so fair, and his stern resolve droops and saddens. Does mine as well? I'm certain of it.

I feel my composure shrivel around the edges as I think back to when I had a big sister and best friend. I haven't thought of missing her in so long. We didn't have a double wedding…too show biz for Papa…but we might have. And then it seemed so quickly to end. My cherished Mimi bled to death, so happy to be pregnant, and I went on without my best friend, fulfilling my wifely duty at each new year, then losing my resolve as my belly grew, and each September delivering another child, whose name could not begin with A, and every year learning how to be happy in spite of things that might not be as I had dreamed. I cannot bear to think how different my life might have been if Anne-Marie had lived to keep me from my cynical self. She shared her sweetness, little imagining how much I needed it.

Montreal

On a trip to Québec after my father died, I went to visit Robin and Carman Bradley, who had been at McGill University with Étienne.

Étienne had rented a room for three years from Ivy Wright, Robin's mother, before getting his own apartment. Ivy's husband had left when Robin was nine years old, and to make ends meet, Ivy would lease a room in her tidy house in lower Westmount to a McGill student, who was expected to help with the coal furnace and the snow shovelling. On meeting Étienne, Ivy decided she had better rent out a second room to a second student. Étienne, though charming, did not appear to be the shovelling type. In fact, Ivy joked that he looked like he expected to have his clothes laid out for him. (We knew our father to be the shovelling type, but do not know whether he changed in response to Ivy's assessment of him, or whether he just came to embrace a more rugged life.)

Robin and Étienne started McGill in the fall of 1951, when he was already twenty-four years old. In his Geology courses he met Jo, my mother.

Robin showed me some pictures from her old McGill yearbooks. Étienne belonged to the Outdoors Club. Jo was a Winter Carnival Queen runner-up. One summer, Ivy suggested Étienne get a job, so he got one selling encyclopedias door-to-door, made his quota in a week, then spent the rest of the summer in the Rockies. In 1954 Robin and Carman left McGill and married. While they sat in the cold railway station, waiting for the train taking them to their honeymoon in Lake Placid, a bubbly party was going on up the hill, fueled by a case of champagne provided by Étienne. After their daughter, Brenda, was born, the Bradleys moved to Calgary and lived with Carman's parents. Étienne became Brenda's godfather. Étienne and Jo, not yet married, moved to Alberta a year later. They got together a few times for dinner. Then in 1957, before I was born, the Bradleys returned to Montreal, and lost track of Étienne when he remarried some years later.

Almost a life

Silent Super 8 movies from the late nineteen-fifties and early nineteen-sixties add substance to a life. We've receded so far from that shore that in my mind that life seems small, ambiguous, not just in space but in time, reduced to a few photos, some dim memories, and random bits of reminiscing. But when we pick up the telescope, or simply stop looking through the wrong end, the scene expands, inflates like a balloon, round and graspable.

My father was usually the one behind the camera. A notable exception was a clip of him loping around the back yard throwing a ball for my mother's German Shepherd. He was in his early thirties then, without a hint of the back trouble that would come to plague him, without his usual disdain for pet dogs. "Another girl?", Dad had said when Jackie was born. The dog may have been an outlet for the rambunction that he couldn't imagine in his three daughters.

These short films record an equally short marriage, at their home on 7th St in Calgary, and at their cottage at St. Donat in the Laurentians. It was a different life from the one Étienne left in France, and different again from the life he led when he first came to Alberta to work in the oil business, living in a trailer in the bush in a place marked on the topographic maps of the time as Tank, but which became

Peace River. Whether pushed or pulled, he left the bush for a settled, even polished, life in Calgary and turned his attention to investing in real estate.

Chinook

The Chinook (Cree for Snow Melter), a weather event particular to the rain shadow in the lee of the high mountains, is the Calgarian's reward for hard winters, and is as magical as it is unpredictable. West winds, pressed down the mountainsides onto the plain, warm rapidly (twenty-one degrees in four minutes is Alberta's record), melting snow and ice and hard countenances. It is often heralded by a chinook arch, the sharp-edged arc of cloud revealing the spotless blue sky behind it, more rainbow than rain in meaning.

Étienne owned a charter flight service and flying school in Calgary, named after those favourable mountain winds. Flying put the ranch within easy reach, however he inherited an early hearing loss which ended his flying career. It was so many years ago that he sold the last of his Piper Twin Comanche airplanes that it's easy to discount the importance flying had in his life.

I was about five years old when I flew with my father in one of his planes. We had flown commercially back and forth to Montreal to visit family, eleven hours on Trans Canada Airlines' Vanguards, but a small plane was entirely different, and my only memory of the trip was terror. Dad banked steeply so that when I looked out the window beside me, I was looking at the ground. I screamed. He laughed.

"You were never in danger. That's just how an airplane turns." I'm putting words in his mouth. What else can I do with him gone and my memories fraying? Whatever might have been said, I was not frightened to get back on a big plane. Just nervous. Just not too adventurous. I came to think of that flight as a lesson in character building, a lesson I failed. It was probably nothing of the sort, but such unintentional lessons continued, mostly on four wheels; Dad drove at autobahn speeds and passed big rigs, playing chicken, leaving us swaying and white-knuckled in the back seat. Before he had children to bounce around the back of a station wagon, he was legendary for tearing up speeding tickets when caught out of province, driving long distances without sleep, even once spending a night in jail in some town in Québec.

None of his children inherited his passion for flight. However, I always loved the view from an airplane window, especially the furrowed, tanned skin of the western drift plains, and always, on returning to Toronto, the first sight of Lake Ontario's shimmer, the first breath of humid air that said 'home'. Flying has become not pedestrian, but bus-like, cheap, no more chinaware, flatware, glassware, full meals, tiny liquor bottles, space, equanimity. I still feel the cheap thrill; the big thrill frightened out of me; the vestige of fright never reasoned out of me.

Gravel Roads

NO GASOLINE OR
TOURIST FACILITIES
NEXT 109 km

I recall as a child driving to the ranch, that when we left the paved highway east of Calgary and headed into the Palliser Triangle, it was nearly two hours on gravel roads, with the constant tumble of gravel against the bottom of the truck, and a great plume of dust, visible for miles, bringing up the rear. The truck in question was most often, or perhaps just most fondly recalled, the school bus yellow GMC Suburban. Radio reception thinned out to nothing and there were only our briefly exchanged words embroidering the tinny racket. We bumped and jostled along on faith and a full tank of gas. There were few signs, few places to announce, few landmarks, especially for the too-young-to-drive. It was a sea, and one wouldn't look for signs or landmarks on the sea, but on land such looking was natural. In a truck, you can't read the land as you might on foot. Where are we? Are we lost? Am I lost in a memory, missing the landmarks of shared recollection? We had only to look out the window of the Suburban at the white-hot sky and the featureless plain to know there was no point in asking "are we there yet?" Eventually the road ran along a railroad track and grain elevators would rise and then sink from view, announcing Rosemary, Duchess, Patricia, Iddesleigh, Jenner, Altee. Turn left in the middle of nowhere and you've arrived!

Ranches

A big farm table with an amusing lazy-susan, a shallow stream filled with cobbles and shaded by small trees, stepping into a trailer then frozen to the spot at the sight of the floor covered with mousetraps, pinning tiny lumps of fur—those were my first child-sized views of a thing called ranch. The ranch in question was called Kentucky Ranch and was in the foothills of the Rocky Mountains near High River, Alberta. My father bought it after I was born, in the late nineteen-fifties or early nineteen-sixties with money from his father, and sold some years later, simply too small for my father's ambit.

He bought a bigger—much bigger—ranch in the Palliser Triangle, dry and far from anything, coloured the palest yellow on maps. Not worth a nickel, much of it abandoned.

Buying this ranch was a picking up of pieces, assembling a ranch of exploited, abandoned, clung to, hopefully homesteaded quarter-sections and the native grasses themselves, known to beasts and nations that had been driven to oblivion, once free of imagined property lines, boundaries, fences, iron rails. This land, like all land, looked like freedom, but was equally fetters and false hope. My father named it Majestic.

The Crown and the Canadian Pacific Railway extended their

reach across the emptied plains, invoking sovereignty, a made-up story that had been bronzed and burnished over centuries into hard currency, hollow at its core. An equally imaginary grid was overlaid on the prairie and 160-acre quarter sections practically given away to adventurous settlers who trekked overland or later followed the railroad in the late eighteen-hundreds and early nineteen-hundreds. The homestead map of southern Alberta resembled acres of square stockyard pens, as much prison as opportunity. Canvas towns like Medicine Hat sprang up along the tracks to collect, direct, and serve the new settlers. The CPR was the company store to which settlers were held captive.

Majestic had been a railroad siding, one of dozens laid out every ten miles along the Bassano Subdivision line, a single track running east from Bassano, Alberta to Saskatchewan, opened by the CPR in 1914. The sidings became towns, part towns, ghost towns, planned-but-never-built towns. Some ended as they'd started, with only a sign bearing its name.

They were named by the CPR for members of the British royal family and their hangers-on, perhaps those whose pockets the CPR had picked. From Empress to Countess, the rail line and its wooden grain elevators were abandoned within a hundred years. Majestic was a water stop for the steam locomotives, which needed to take on water every fifty miles or so. A man who lived miles off down by the Red Deer River, would keep the forty-thousand-gallon reservoir filled, pump water up to the siding, then he would settle back to whatever he did living alone, gardening on the floodplain up against a coulee. The rhubarb he had planted still grows, untended, but the reservoir is empty, the huge pump rusted into silence.

The first and lasting impressions of the Majestic ranch were the aching silence that made flies sound like airplanes, the dead and silenced flies littering the tables, counters, windowsills in the trailer, the mute landscape itself, a nearly unbroken horizon, the constant wind barely a whisper.

When asked why he traded a welcoming and sheltering ranch in the foothills for a ranch in the featureless semi-desert, Mr. B. replied that the cows don't care about the scenery. In 1969 he hired Si and Marg Schonhofer from Bar Pipe Ranch, another foothills spread. Marg did care about the scenery, and everything it bespoke; she cried for two years. When they arrived, there were 475 head of cattle, but no irrigation, no equipment, no cash flow, four young children and the nearest doctor seventy-five miles away on dirt roads that were impassable quagmires when it rained.

Mr. B. offered Si not just a job, but shares in the ranch, "so he wouldn't be inclined to leave wrenches out in the rain to rust".

The Schonhofers first occupied the small farm at the upper buildings. They kept a cow for milk and butter, chickens for eggs and meat, and Marg made her own bread. To all of us children raised in the city, this was quaintly rustic and admirably self-sufficient. To them this was a necessity. There was no store to dash off to when something ran out. In one of the early dry years, before the irrigation systems were installed, hay had to be shipped in from elsewhere in the province. When we asked why, Mr. B. replied, "I can't send the cows to the store with a quarter".

The lower buildings included a blacksmith shop, once a necessity but now long abandoned, and a small, sad, derelict shed heaped with an eyepopping number of Playboy magazines. Touring the ranch again in 1996, a few years before he sold it, Mr. B. pointed out the lower buildings from the crest of a coulee. They now included feeding pens for three thousand head of cattle, pivot irrigation, a big mechanical shop, hopper bins, a truck scale, and trailers with satellite TV for the hired help.

Scattered over the whole were a handful of farmsteads abandoned in the nineteen-thirties. The names Bullen, Hayes, Gordon, Donaldson can be discerned on the old hand-drawn homestead maps from 1918. Who built and then walked away from these worn, colourless houses?

When we first visited the ranch as children, we were offered rifles to try our hand at shooting... tin cans off old foundation walls but also (mercifully) mostly missed gophers, an early lesson in distinguishing 'pests' from the rest of life. Shooting was another of the adventures shared by my parents. Amongst my mother's paraphernalia were Dominion of Canada Marksman pins. The Dominion of Canada Rifle Association still exists, a poor cousin to the American National Rifle Association. Marksmanship was undoubtedly a vestige of WWII patriotism that became a badge of Western belonging.

We were always told to wear boots outside at the ranch because there were rattlesnakes, though Mr. B. had been known to go outside in bedroom slippers. We'd never seen rattlers around the house, and in any case if any lurked there, they could effortlessly strike your leg above a boot. To catch sight of rattlesnakes involved a long drive to a particular coulee, where they were known to den. Stepping slowly and carefully down the steep slopes we spotted them coiled in the sun. Sometimes, there was no sign of them until someone picked up and tossed a handful of gravel. Then you could discern a warning rattle there... and there!

Another coulee was the deadstock graveyard. Though much of the original settlers' horse drawn machinery was left where it was abandoned, slowly being buried by the drifted silt, larger trucks, tractors, and equipment that no longer served a purpose were tipped downslope and left to rust in a jumble.

Burning Down the House

O ne night, I burned a stash of my old love letters that I'd been saving for years, occasionally pulling them out and savouring their flavour, until I lost my taste for them. The paper burned dangerously hot and left crumpled black ash flowers.

The act itself made me think of my father on the day of my mother's funeral. He seemed uncharacteristically upset and asked to have one of the old photographs of her on display. She was once a beautiful, young, spirited woman; he confessed to having burned all his photos of her when she'd left him. I'd never seen such attachment in him. She'd flamed out, crumpling his orderly life. I suppose they were quite a pair once, impossibly long ago.

One imagines burning photos and letters as I did it, in an old-fashioned fireplace, the fire the only light in the room, and insufficient to penetrate the corners, a glass of wine at hand, perhaps. In Dad's case the glass of wine could well have been a gin and tonic, clean, cut with an edge of anger. Photography was an early hobby of his and he must have had a sizable collection of photographs, now lost. Far less romantic, but equally possible in those days, would have been to chuck the stacks of photographs into the trash-burning can in the back alley, watch them melt and mottle, blister and curl, crackle and shrivel into a reptilian skin, making acrid black smoke to match his mood.

"Do you think we put enough kerosene on that?" Mr. B.'s words ring out clearly on the videotape. It's a winter day at the ranch, snow on the barren ground around an old farmhouse, abandoned in the dust bowl years and now grey and lifeless as the winter sky.

Flames rush around the corner of the house, through the doorframe, as if being blown from a torch. More kerosene? What a sense of humour. Steam from the melting snow swirls around the foundation, evoking the lost souls who lived and died there. Smoke pours from the roof, first white and then raging black, tall, fierce, frightening.

The old house, one of several abandoned farmsteads on the ranch, needed to come down, Mr. B. asserted, to prevent its collapsing and injuring a cow. All those who had joined him in this spectacle knew this was a flimsy excuse for an adventure, man's—and I do mean man's—affinity for playing with fire. The neighbours and what municipal services existed were notified. Smoke from the fire would have been visible for miles. But no-one needed to come save lives, and there would have been no hope of saving even a valued building. Vestiges of settlers' lives entered the soil, joining the bison and Plains people. The past is in the earth, the future, over the next hummock.

The Cattle Auction

The camera pans crowds of cowboy hats filling one side of a Quonset hut on the ranch. On the other side there's a dirt-floored pen and a raised stage. Si Schonhofer, the ranch manager, wearing a ballcap with the Majestic Ranches LIX brand on the front, welcomes everyone and says a few words about the cattle that are on offer, bred heifers—all pregnancy tested. Mr. B. steps forward in a watch cap and puffy jacket, nods his head slightly, and is introduced as the partner who writes the cheques and pays the bills. This is Si's show.

A dozen white-faced heifers, their backs-sugar coated with snow, enter the pen and mill and churn until their heads are together in the centre of the swirl, the prey animal instinct strangely recalling the ballet chorus of Swan Lake.

The guest soloist is the auctioneer, in a dazzling white Stetson and jacket. He launches into his incomprehensible and rapid-fire coaxing of dollars from pockets. He raises his hand, points a finger, nods his head, and occasionally, surprisingly, breaks into a loping understandable English in Hank Snow tones, extolling the virtues of these cattle;

"these are all range cattle,

come right in off the coulees,

they know how to look after themselves."

A cowboy in the pen extends his authority over the cows with a crooked staff, waving and pointing, but with one eye on the crowd of buyers. His fingers flash, he exclaims in monosyllables, "ho" and "hi", looking like a conductor in an orchestra pit.

As mysteriously as it started, the bidding ends and the lot is hammered down. Sold! The ladies smartly exit the pen stage left, making room for the next lot.

Prairie Oysters

E
ven with today's passion for farm-to-table, tail-to-snout dining, you will not likely find Prairie Oysters on any menu.

Prairie Oysters are calf testicles, easy to prepare, but almost impossible to source. They are reportedly like chicken gizzards in consistency and flavour, or for the many of us too young to have encountered chicken gizzards on their plates, they are like liver. That still leaves most in the dark, as organ meats have disappeared from most grocery stores and even the trendiest restaurants need to fancy them up to move them.

As it happens, when your business is livestock, your inventory can walk, run, and be rustled. Thus, every June, the new calves were branded, along with being vaccinated, castrated, and polled, that is, having their horn buds excised.

The 1989 branding at Majestic Ranches was documented on videotape until the camera battery ran out. The film had little dialogue but constant sound. Baaww Baaww Baaww are the bass notes, the calves constantly bawling. The steady roar of the propane burners, heating the branding irons, is white noise. All other sounds are mere patter. The action is repetitive, even boring; excitement is discouraged. The scenery barely changes.

Branding was a three-day campout for fifty or so hands, some handier than others, some professional, some amateur, some hands-on, some supportive. The herd of cows and calves, previously rounded-up, course slowly back and forth between the fences. The ropers on horseback are slow and relaxed. They twirl their lassoes with ease, without sudden movement. The last thing anyone wants is a stampede. There is not a hint of the dust-raising speed and white-eyed terror attendant on rodeo calf-roping.

A rider ropes a calf and drags it from the herd to where wranglers and wrestlers flip and pin it. Cutters, branders, inoculators castrate the males, remove horn buds, give each a shot, mark them with the brand, L I X. Their fur flames and smokes. The whites of their eyes flash beneath long white eyelashes; their white tongues loll from their bawling mouths. Once released they run back to the herd. Five hundred calves might be done in a morning. It is worth remembering that all vocations, no matter how exciting they seem, are built on a broad base of tedium.

As the morning proceeds, fair weather clouds swell in the summer sky. The camera pans the action, rests now and then on irons in the hissing fire, the milk can into which the calves' testicles are dropped, trailing drippy ducts, Mr. B., standing, syringe in hand, his back to the camera (a back that was never up to cowboy stuff), the fence-line behind which sit a line of grownups in lawn chairs, who prefer to watch the action at some remove, along with little children in their Calgary Stampede gear, clean wee vests, blue jeans and cowboy hats, next to a line of pickup trucks and horse trailers.

Not discernable from the film is the smell, the dust in your mouth, the heat, the aching muscles, and fatigue borne of constant vigilance.

When the day's work was done all hands were rewarded with a swim in the river, beer and barbeque, a box full of kites for the kids, and a night full of stars and the sleep of the dead.

Prairie Oysters

Recipe

Remove the testicle from its furry sac. In true tail to snout form, the sacs make attractive Barbie doll hats.

Trim and rinse the testicles and roll them in flour, season with salt and pepper.

Add oil to a cast iron skillet and fry the little balls until they are crispy on the outside.

Serve them from the pan, paired with beer. Please—no artisanal brew—only industrial suds will do.

French Connection

Although my father lived in France for the first twenty years of his life, we did not speak French at home, a lost opportunity to become bilingual. (It was my mother who might have called one of us "*mon petit chou*".) This may have been my father's way to further distance himself from his family of origin. Alberta, where we were born, saw little reason to embrace *francophonie* and did not require school children to learn French, as was the case in Ontario. Visits to Europe with children in tow were rare events.

It seemed the only aspects of his French heritage that my father embraced were wine and good food, though as we grew to adulthood, we realized how unvaried his meals could be and how lacking in vegetables! He favoured tea over coffee, lettuce over sturdy greens; bitterness had no place even on his plate.

Over the years of visits with his siblings in France or Switzerland, he had collected recipes from them, handwritten in French in their fine European script. I don't recall seeing them or enjoying the finished dishes while he was alive, but after he died, they were given to those of us who could read French. Deciphering the handwriting was a bigger hurdle than translating French cooking terms.

There was no recipe for frogs' legs, though we were told that the cook used to hang them from the kitchen porch railings to drain, and that they would 'dance' in the rain. There was no recipe required for cracking eggs into a glass and drinking them raw, which Étienne was known to do. Steak was barely grilled, 'blue' in his terms. Add pâté and cases of full-bodied red wines and you have a recipe for gout, the rich man's disease, which plagued him for years. Étienne favoured smoky Lapsang Souchong tea, burnt toast and the newspaper with breakfast. We learned to love his stinky French cheeses. Once when his sister came to visit, the border inspectors questioned a large half-moon shape on her luggage X-ray. "It's a make-up bag," she replied with intimidating certainty. It was, in fact, a half wheel of Chaumes cheese. Had the suitcase been opened the smell of rotten socks would have elicited equally quick and confident "*au contraire*".

VRAIMENT…

Rösti à la Zürichoise

Gratin Dauphinoise

Crêpes Parmentier

Gâteau peau de lait

Quelles appellations belles!

Vive la cuisine éternelle!

Character(s)

Experimental artist and musician, Laurie Anderson, has proposed that what you do in life should be two of three things: fun, lucrative, interesting—never just one! Étienne usually managed to have all three. He started with many advantages—privilege really—wealth, intelligence, imagination, sense of humour, a repertoire of jokes, a liberal ease with all types of people.

Is Étienne now noisily dragging his chains through the netherworld? What links did he forge in life, a man of business, whose business was not mankind? Did he have regrets that died with him? He took his concept of himself to the other side. He left us with his avatar to which we've stuck labels bearing little descriptions, which fail to make the whole. "Generous but not sharing." "Never has anything serious to say." "Doesn't like to be seen in moments of weakness." "Seems baffled to have ended up with seven children." "A big fish in a small pond." "His only exercise was jumping to conclusions." "Emotionally distant." "You can go out in public in a silly hat but not with a hole in your sweater." All the little pieces come unstuck, fall to the ground, are swept into a pile, dry and curl, swirl and crackle, blow away. We are left with the memory of labels...impressions of impressions.

He did not have much to say about his own parents or siblings. His father spent his leisure time finishing an extensive genealogy of the Burrus family, and several Burruses wrote memoirs, if only for their own descendants. In 1997 a cousin organized an equally extensive family reunion in Alsace. Étienne was as excited as I'd ever seen him to be reunited with his cousins, Jacques and Dominique, the only childhood friends allowed him. He was as uncomfortable as I'd ever seen him at the Mass given by the family, muttering that he had not been inside a church since his father's funeral in 1974. I write this at Christmas and wonder if Étienne, sitting in a cathedral for what would have been the last time, thought differently about what his Catholic lessons really meant; that he might have a different way of explaining the mystery of Christmas to his grandchildren than the silence his children got on the topic. Did he still doubt such a man as Jesus (or Mohammed, or Buddha) might have walked the Earth, might have had lessons to teach?

Now when I read, I pay close attention to character development, especially to those characters who do not let themselves be known. Perhaps fiction would be a means to make Étienne more definite, solid. But I can't be unequivocal. That's not how it was.

Yet I do imagine that as the youngest of four boys, Étienne yearned to travel far, to the west of North America, to be his own person and away from the shadows of his family. He had two older sisters, Françoise and Anne-Marie, who married industrialists from the north of France and settled into the lives for which they had been raised, though Anne-Marie died young. His younger sister, Agnès, did anything but settle, her favourite residence being an airplane going somewhere else. Françoise judged her brothers to be turbulent additions to an idyllic family, inspiring their father's wrath, creating a stormy atmosphere in a once peaceful home. Martin was difficult but original and loved the mountains, dying at forty during a rescue mission in the Colorado Rockies. Bernard was valorous and flamboyant, even a "*flambeur*". René was more reserved, a steady hand, and though younger than Bernard, inherited the directorship of the family firm.

The parents doted on their children, offered them little freedom, fostered no friendships, made them conform; such was the style then. These restrictions did not prevent the children from creating their own world of fun, animated by Anne-Marie's imagination and Martin's eccentricity. When the fun became outrageous or perhaps merely unseemly, their father exploded in stentorian rage.

Not much in life made Étienne angry; there was likely no room for more anger in his father's house. If only Étienne had been able to express what he didn't like, he might have been able to make changes to his relationships instead of withdrawing from them.

The last family photo in which Étienne appears, is that of his parents' fiftieth wedding anniversary in 1961. He was thirty-four years old, attending alone, his first marriage secretly on the rocks. Of the thirty-five people in the photo only Étienne and a handful of his young nephews and nieces are smiling frankly, the rest wear the slight smiles or straight faces that characterized most Burrus family photographs. No hearts on sleeves!

Those of his siblings who visited the ranch loved the excitement, though certainly none, including Étienne himself, would have wanted to live in such splendid isolation. They were impressed by his success. He was a pilot, a marksman, a hiker and skier, adventurous— but within bounds. A trip to Southeast Asia in the nineteen-nineties that involved stays in less-than-two-star accommodations, unfamiliar foods and cultures was outside his comfort level, though he never admitted that. He found a reasonably plausible excuse to need to be in Mexico and never regretted missing the trip.

I remember seeing a photograph of Dad at the head of the table, carving a turkey, and mingling with the shock of realizing I had no memory of spending Christmas with him, was the dismay of seeing him rather casually dressed. Christmas in my mother's family was a formal occasion, jackets and ties, dresses and sparkly jewellery. In the photo, though the family sat among polished mahogany and silver in the grand house in Calgary, there was a sense of occasion missing.

I suppose dressing up was one of the things Étienne left behind when he left Europe. While he embraced a bit of exotica—a guayabera and sombrero, a buckskin suit tailor-made from a hunting trophy, a folk costume bought at a market in Guatemala, an Elvis costume, complete with chest hairs dyed black with mascara—he was not a clothes horse. In a photo from early days with my mother, he is caught mid-sentence, finger raised to make a point, wearing outrageously mismatched floral swim trunks and a plaid shirt, which my mother undoubtedly found hilarious, possibly endearing. Decidedly unceremonious. When my mother first brought Étienne home to meet the family, she tried to re-dress her teenaged brother, Vic, and add some style to the occasion. She needn't have bothered. A few years later, when Vic went to Calgary to attend my parent's small wedding at the Palliser Hotel, he recalled Étienne pointing out a grubbily dressed man among the suits in the lobby and telling him that it was the way of the west that Mr. Shabby may well have been the richest man there.

His obituary focused on fun and on his dream of becoming a cowboy. He did not have any affinity for plants or animals, did not study agriculture like his brother who went on to buy an *orangerie* in Morocco. Yet by hiring the right people and being well-capitalized, he made a success of ranching the dry-land prairie. A newspaper clipping from 1961, when he won an award for the highest marks on his flying exams, identified Étienne as "a Longview rancher". I imagine this secretly pleased him. (It would have been my mother who cut out the article for her scrapbook, though she thought herself the better pilot of the two.)

He was a person of integrity, which accords with his oldest

sister's assessment of him as someone incapable of telling a lie. He was fair and felt it his duty to pass on his inheritance, though money didn't mean much to him. He liked a bargain but was not miserly. He was generous when asked for something but didn't offer, whether that something was cash, advice, or guidance. He would defer to his children's wishes in disputes involving maternal advice or guidance.

His friend, Hugh, wrote to us in his role as Étienne's executor, that our father was "a man from a different age, a different cultural set, a different social, economic, political era, and from a different emotional backdrop" and that this, along with his hearing loss, was why Étienne sometimes seemed distant. "We men were raised not to cry, to be stoic, to be fearless, at least outwardly." We sons and daughters were, in our silent grieving, to treasure the thought that his estate was "an outlet for his love for you all."

Étienne further guarded his distance with drink: a case of champagne for the Bradley's wedding while still at McGill, a bottle of rye to accompany reviewing the ranch bills once a month with Si, a mickey of gin to mix hair-raising gin and tonics at the end of a day's road trip. Drink tapped into his repertoire of jokes, his ease at sitting down (untaught) to a piano or with a guitar and playing and singing, his willingness to engage in costumed frivolity.

The Indigenous view, as expressed by the Cree playwright Tomson Highway, is that life is about laughter. Fun. The trickster is at the core of everything. Étienne ended up traveling with the trickster, his protector, without realizing it.

The hardest thing is to conjure an image of him. While he inherited the family gene for early hearing loss, he did not get the gene for hair loss. His dark hair kept him looking as young as he acted. As a young man he was thin, boney, handsome in his way with careful brown eyes that did not betray his thoughts or emotions. He joked he had a Roman nose, "roamin' all over his face", but that was more amusement than truth. His bad back and stiff gait reinforced each other. His English was perfect, but a little too perfect to pass as a native English speaker. He did not speak French to us—a mark of how far he wanted to distance himself from his origins.

Fresh Connections

I am...

Since Étienne didn't speak of himself much, I didn't wonder how he would complete that phrase.

Though Étienne was far from a practising Catholic, he became godfather to his Montreal landlady's first granddaughter, Brenda. Her parents, Robin and Carman, were also McGill pals. To Brenda, Étienne was a seldom seen and mythical creature. Forty years later, when they had reconnected only for the second time, he offered this biographical sketch to Brenda in an email:

"I am now 71 years old, have been in the oil business (who hasn't in this burg?) then owned a charter air business and flying school, then a fairly large ranch for the last 30 years. Just sold it to my faithful manager of 30 years ... couldn't bear to sell it to somebody else and put him out in the cold night.

I spend the warm seasons between Calgary and Victoria B.C., and the cold winters at my condo in Mexico on the Pacific Coast, golfing, deep-sea fishing, and exploring archaeological sites, (illegally) looking for Toltec and Aztec artifacts."

Their first connection had been a quarter-century earlier when Brenda was sixteen. Étienne was in Montreal and had dinner with Brenda's parents and asked what special thing she might like for her sixteenth birthday. It was also the year of his mother's death, and while in Alsace sitting in the church in Ste. Croix, it may have occurred to him that he not only had a goddaughter but had some duty to her that he had neglected. While that should have involved inquiring after her Catholic upbringing, and while Brenda's parents hoped for practical assistance with books or clothes, Étienne had less pedestrian ideas. How about a motorbike? A few months later, a shiny red Honda 100 was delivered.

Then Étienne disappeared again.

When they reconnected, the biographical sketch was followed up with an offer of a few flying lessons, or perhaps some parachute lessons? Here he was dipping into his past, painting Brenda in the same tints that had coloured my mother, another adventurous Montrealer. My mother also had a motorbike, also took flying lessons.

The Cattle Drive

My last visit to the ranch was in the summer of 1996, two years before Mr. B. sold it. The local news was full of a ninety km. cattle drive from Buffalo to Medicine Hat across Canadian Forces Base Suffield, a mostly unfenced weapons testing range. This event was a re-creation of one of the original drives of longhorns from Texas into Alberta, in celebration of the one hundredth anniversary of the Western Stock Growers' Association.

A different cattle drive, organized by Cochrane Ranche Co. near Calgary in the late eighteen-hundreds, brought six to seven thousand head north from the western states at a murderous pace of twelve to eighteen miles a day, managed by thirty cowboys and three hundred horses. Hundreds of cows weakened and died on the trail, and hundreds more died between Calgary and Cochrane when winter set in before the herd could reach shelter and water. The fate of the men and horses on the Cochrane drive is left to the imagination; cowboys were famously stoic and uncomplaining. Their getting hired depended not only on their horse and rope skills, but also on their reputation for following orders and not causing trouble, habits many acquired in the American Confederate or Union armies.

The very first cattle drives were herds of hardy longhorn,

descended from cattle brought by the Spaniards into Texas and later the northern plains territories. The cattle filled the prairie emptied of bison and were driven annually to the few railheads to be shipped east to market. These cattle drives were less brutal; minimizing the daily costs for cowboys, horses and their feed had to be balanced against maintaining the herd's health and weight and market value.

The 1996 cattle drive, re-enacted in celebratory fashion, involved almost as many humans as cows. Two thousand head of cattle, fifteen hundred people, seventeen hundred horses and mules, one hundred wagons and carriages and ten volunteer veterinarians made the trip at nine to twelve miles a day.

Hot showers, catered meals, beer wagons, and other comforts unheard of a hundred years ago, offset the toll taken by hot dry weather, nervous cattle, renegade horses, broken bones, saddle sores, foot rot, broken gear, and enthusiastic inexperience. Equally unprepared were a group of camouflaged British soldiers, prone on the ground in the dark, who suddenly found themselves in danger of being trampled by wayward cowboys riding through in search of wayward animals.

Cattle drive-lite continues to be a feature of the Calgary Stampede and Alberta dude ranch tourism in general. The golden age of the cowboy was barely a generation, from the time that the end of the American Civil War released hundreds of young men into the west, to the late eighteen-hundreds when cattle barons and their great herds were whittled down by overgrazing, depressed cattle prices, the spread of settled town life, and the increasingly fenced range. The cowboy sat tall in the saddle for only a few moments of the history of the west but cast a long and fantastical shadow.

Driven

the cattle drive proceeds apace
the horses are already gone,
replaced with metal machines,
eyeless, breathless

the skies are not cloudy all day
and the river wizens between muddy banks
those green pastures must be over the hill
where the future becomes the present

for now, follow the great herds of bison
into the past, into the dust
that explodes as each hoof
strikes the dry earth

A Presence

It was 1956. Étienne was working in the bush in the Peace River district of Alberta at a place identified on maps only as Tank. Jo had followed him west. I imagine their relationship was as wild as the new petrochemical frontier. But back then, birth control was only available to women who were married, so Jo relied on a fatalistic mix of denial and miscarriage. As each pregnancy lasted longer, denial's false front crumbled. In the end the three thousand miles between her family and her gravid condition kept her baby's birth a secret. She gave her baby the only gift she could—the name Stephanie—and gave her away. Three months later, our parents' volatile relationship was sanctified, and three more baby girls followed in close succession before the marital house of cards collapsed. Mom brought us back east when Dad remarried.

Mom told us the secret of Stephanie when we were still in elementary school. The secret came out for good at mom's funeral in 2002. Her own siblings heard the story for the first time, at once amazed and saddened. Dad was at the funeral, too. He tried, tentatively, to cast doubt on his paternity. We politely refrained from reminding him that the baby had been named after him.

Stephanie appeared in our lives in 2004, under her own

name—Lyn. The first cell phone photo showed her to be unmistakably our father's daughter. Dad embraced this new reality with his usual gracious, if slightly uncertain, aplomb.

Like a drop of blue ink in a white dish of water we all became a family without fanfare, flowing with the grace that water embodies. The blue ink spreads until there is no ink and no water, only blue. Perhaps by standing for nothing, Dad stood for everything. Was that his teaching, viral and without intent, delivered in the end with a laugh?

Grave Goods

Diplomat German Typewriter

This typewriter was one of seven collected by Étienne for use in various office spaces, or perhaps in the case of a used Smith Corona Coronamatic Electric bought two years before he died, to be cannibalized for parts in the diminishing world of typewriter sales and service. Étienne brought this particular typewriter from France, perhaps after his father's death. A keyboard with German characters would have been of little use when he first immigrated to Montreal in the nineteen-fifties, though its use was at least necessary in Switzerland where the family business was domiciled, and at most mandatory in occupied Alsace during World War II. The stencilled "4" indicated it may have come from an F.J. Burrus & Cie office steno pool. Étienne likely arrived in Montreal and McGill University with his quaint Corona Special folding typewriter in hand. One of his Smith Corona typewriters was touted as being "built to last and produce neat results with ease." These features of typewriters would have appealed to Étienne's sensibilities and values. He grew up in a house in which not only his father, but his mother, had an office, and in which domestic life was orderly and businesslike.

Austrian "Franz Joseph" 100 Corona Coin

One of several such coins Étienne owned, it was also brought from France on his father's death. His father reputedly bought them during World War II as a hedge against societal breakdown, though as dual citizens the family had managed to obtain permission to travel to Switzerland, a neutral country, where they remained until the war's end. These gold coins, each an ounce of pure gold, originally commemorated the diamond jubilee of Austro-Hungarian Emperor Franz Joseph I in 1915, though they were restruck many times in the ensuing years with the same 1915 date to get around the depression era US prohibition of private gold ownership. The reverse of the coin bears the Austro-Hungarian Empire's coat of arms, a double-headed eagle with the Hapsburg Dynasty shield. The obverse shows a profile of Franz Joseph I, and the edge of the coin is inscribed with his personal motto, *"Unitas Viribus"*, "with united force". Franz Joseph was revered for his great power as a leader and the coins bearing his image conveyed stability, strength and integrity when times were anything but. For a time in his later years, Étienne lost track of his stash of Franz Josephs. He eventually found them in a box of staples, pushing them aside and asking, "so then where are the staples?"

Briefcase

This leather briefcase with metal findings was the most classic of a collection of briefcases—boxy or elegant, leather or aluminum—used sequentially and simultaneously by Étienne. Such satchels and cases were needed before pockets had been added to clothing. Now briefcases themselves have pockets to appeal to the neat and orderly mind. Luxury leather goods were for those more extravagant than Étienne. This particular case bears no brand or subtle logo, just a well-hidden tag saying, "crafted in China". Étienne carried neither briefs nor attachés but would have transported documents between his various office spaces. At least one briefcase always accompanied him on trips, even those for pleasure, as a means for organizing various currencies, maps, hotel bills. So ubiquitous were Étienne's briefcases that on his death it was thought fitting to place his ashes in one of them, and in this way, he was present at his own memorial service and transported to his own ash-scattering ceremony at the ranch.

The French Exit

You left the party without saying goodbye, Dad.

By 2006 the doctors' appointments were becoming more frequent and concerning. We daughters of marriage number one were talking about coming to Calgary to spend Christmas with you, something we had only done in an unremembered past. When Jackie returned from a business trip in November and asked you what had happened at a recent doctor's appointment, you said "Well, they told me to go into a little room, take off my clothes and put on a gown..."

A few days later, Jackie arranged by phone to have lunch with you and Kay in two weeks.

"I won't be there; you can have lunch with Kay."

"Where are you going to be?"

No answer. What a comedian. There were no travel plans at this stage, and the ranch, sold years ago, was no longer a bolthole.

"Okay, Dad, see you soon"

This Jackie did. The next day you collapsed, unconscious, some undisclosed encephalopathy perhaps. By the time the ambulance arrived you had revived and though your colour was bad, could answer the important questions: "what is your name, what day is it?" The querying paramedics brought you to the hospital. There, you handed Kay your glasses.

"I won't be needing these."

You blacked out again, this time for good. Kay and Jackie held your icy hands. The heart is the last to go, you know.

We all went to Calgary for your memorial celebration, the venue, bar, and catering not much different from your and Kay's wedding, three years earlier. You were there too, your ashes resting in irony in one of your briefcases. We talked for days about you, yet I felt as much in the dark as I had while you were still with us. What was I missing; what had I missed? The end for all of us is dark.

The following summer there was another memorial at the ranch. All the old ranch pastimes were replayed and frozen in photographs; flying kites, grilling steaks, shooting tin cans, even giving the old Suburban, patched and pocked but still in use, a slap on the hood. The singular act of the weekend was tossing your ashes in the summer breeze. They fell into the startlingly green grass. I see you still when I see the prairie—all horizon. Though you, too, are gone the way of the bison, you are there in the grass, you are the grass, the prairie, the past.

As If Through a Window

November is the barrens
the tundra of the year,
the lay of the land
suddenly made plain.

November is the Somme
and Ypres of the year,
cold and wet,
muddy and futile.

The emptied forests
and littered gardens,
the silence
of the coming snow

expose you
to the rest of life,
leave you exposed
to the dead.

The prevailing sadness
blows the cloud cover
not away, but in,
bows your head to the wind.

Mia Burrus

What were your dying
thoughts, the ones I never got?
The tunnel with
the brilliant light

at the end, the angels
made perhaps by snuffed
synaptic connections,
the things untold

the cold, cold hand
I didn't get
to hold, the bells
untolled, now the grief

that dribbles out
from my pen,
recalling the first time
I took note

of your spidery script
and senseless sentences.
I am as much in the dark
as before you died.

The Window

I am standing at the window, and not just looking through it, but seeing myself in it. This looking back and looking ahead is about seeing clearly, not through the haze of longing and regret and doubt. It's about seeing myself, the one who is longing, regretting, doubting.

Je me mire et me vois ange! et je meurs, et j'aime
-Que la vitre soit l'art, soit la mysticité

–Les Fenêtres, Mallarmé

leached of blood red tones

the sturdy stones

cannot be breached—the setting

sun's beyond the body's

reach—but not the mind's—

if you can keep that window

shining clean a lifetime's sunsets

always gleam

Mallarmé's windows were in a hospital, struck red-gold by the evening sun—the end of a day—the end of a life. But the sun always rises again. The end is always the beginning.

Inspirations and References

This project was kickstarted by Cynthia Reyes' memoir writing workshop and developed on a trip across the prairies on VIA Rail's Vancouver to Toronto train, a moving feast of a writing retreat!

The epigraph in Making a Killing is by Louise Halfe Sky Dancer, from an untitled poem in Blue Marrow, 4th Ed., Kegedonce Press 2020

The photo in Chinook is the prairie north of Lethbridge, Alberta taken Dec. 2023 by Brian Vasseur from his airplane.

The poem in The Window was first published by me in What I Don't Know, Glentula Press 2021

Burrus Family histories by Jacques Burrus and Françoise Burrus (my father's cousin and sister, respectively) were rich sources of fascinating details.

Brenda Bradley wisely preserved and kindly shared correspondence from her godfather.

My siblings, Lyn, Glenn, Vicky, Jackie, Rob, Cathy, my French cousin Patrick, my uncle Vic and my father's true love, Kay Holt, shared a kaleidoscope of memories, stories, photos, home movies and mementos.

Felicity Sidnell-Reid spent untold hours with me workshopping the pieces and reading the whole.

Étienne and Jo, my parents, gave me a life in which to be curious, create, struggle, and find meaning, for which I am deeply grateful.

Étienne Burrus

May 25, 1927

November 28, 2006

Mia Burrus lives in the country north of Cobourg, Ontario in a restored one-room schoolhouse, where she writes and creates collage/bricolage. She has published a poetry chapbook, <u>What I Don't Know,</u> and several of her artworks were chosen for recent juried shows at local galleries. Visit her own gallery, www.miaburrus.com .

www.ingramcontent.com/pod-product-compliance
Lightning Source LLC
Chambersburg PA
CBHW071215120626
46546CB00006B/2572